AN INTRODUCTION TO WOMEN IN THE BIBLE

AMANDA BEDZRAH

You are loved!

Amanda Bedzrah

EVELYN HOUSE PUBLISHING

CONTENTS

PART TWO

WOMEN IN THE NEW TESTAMENT

WOMEN IN THE NEW TESTAMENT   53
Matthew - Revelation

PART THREE

THE LIAR

When God put it on my heart to do a brief introduction to women in the Bible, I had no idea I would eventually compile a book about them. It started as a fun idea, to do a weekly Facebook Live video where I would introduce some women in the Bible, sharing a brief introduction to the stories of their lives.

My plan was to start from Genesis, all the way to Revelation and share precious nuggets about each woman. The vision I had for the series was to get people so interested in the lives of these women that they would be encouraged to open the Bible and read their stories for themselves. I thought I would have a small audience of people watching the series live with me each week; my heart's desire was to bring the Bible to life through storytelling.

I was not prepared for the impact this series had on people's lives. I was in awe as I received messages and calls thanking me and encouraging me to carry on, telling me how much the series had blessed them and encouraged them to read the Bible. I was humbled at how God could take something that appeared so little to me and use it to change lives.

Over eight weeks, I was able to introduce over 100 women in the Bible. I must stress that I have not covered every one of the women in the Bible. I chose women who I felt had a story to tell or some details about their lives that I could share, and some had more than others.

This book was born out of that series in response to requests by many of the viewers. I hope that it blesses you and that you use it as a simple tool to help you navigate the lives of these incredible women. Although the Bible was written over 2,000 years ago, it is still relevant today; there is so much that we can learn from these women in the Bible.

I have included a short fiction story of a woman in the Old Testament at the end of this book; her story is fascinating. Although she is unnamed in the Bible, I found her name through research in Jewish History. Her name is Zuleika. I hope you enjoy reading it as much as I enjoyed writing it.

I pray that this book will encourage you to open the main book - THE BIBLE - and that as you discover these women for yourselves, God will speak to you and your personal situation.

I pray also that you will find answers to your own questions, comfort, and encouragement from the lives of these women.

Furthermore, I pray that you will be blessed and will find your own story in the stories of these women; in a way that brings deep revelation and meaning to your life.

In Jesus name, Amen.

PS - If you would like to watch the series, it is available on my YouTube Channel: simply type **Amanda Bedzrah** in the YouTube search engine and it will bring up my channel. I would be grateful if you would subscribe to the channel, watch the series, leave comments there or send me a message. Don't forget to share as I am sure there is someone in your world who will be blessed by it.

ACKNOWLEDGMENTS

I am so thankful to my husband and children who are gracious to release me to fulfil God's call on my life. They give me the time and space to research, to pray, to write and to teach. Without their understanding and support, it would have been much harder to be the woman that God has called me to be.

I am also thankful to my sisters, my biggest cheerleaders; and my friends who encourage me and excuse my silence in the seasons of focus and preparation.

My many thanks also to every single person from around the world who has been a part of this journey, especially to those who took the time to reach out to me personally and shared with me the impact of this series on their lives.

I am extremely grateful to the Almighty God for His blessing, His grace, His strength, and this awesome gift He has blessed me with. It does not come without its trials but at every step of the journey, He is consistently with me, leading, guiding and directing me. My life is completely dedicated to the service of God.

To everyone who watched the eight-week series and encouraged me to compile this book.

PART ONE

WOMEN IN THE OLD TESTAMENT

Genesis - Malachi

1. EVE

Genesis 2-4; 2 Corinthians 11:3; and 1Timothy 2:13

The first woman ever created; made out of the rib of her husband, Adam. Eve is mentioned only four times in the Bible: twice in the old Testament and twice in the New Testament.

When deceived by the serpent to disobey God, she encouraged her husband, Adam, to be a part of the disobedience. For this, she is punished in three ways – pain at childbirth, a desire to control her husband, and having her husband rule over her.

2. ADAH AND ZILLAH

Genesis 4:19-23

The wives of Lamech, the first polygamist ever recorded in the Bible, they still managed to live in peace with each other. Lamech both loved and trusted them, something seen when he confessed to them of killing a man who hurt him. We also know that Adah had two sons, Jabal and Jubal, and Zillah had one son, Tubal_-Cain, and one daughter, Naamah.

3. NOAH'S WIFE

Genesis 5:9

Not named in the bible, yet still a significant woman. Loyal and supportive to her husband, Noah, she stood by his side when he spent a hundred years building an ark.

This could not have been easy as they would have both looked like fools to man. Yet the bible stands testimony to Noah's faithfulness in fulfilling God's command, and his wife's commitment in supporting him throughout.

4. NOAH'S DAUGHTERS-IN-LAW

Genesis 5:9 esp 9:1,7,19

Noah's three daughters-in-law are not named in the Bible. The significant fact is, they were in the Ark with Noah, his wife, and their husbands whilst everyone else died.

These three women trusted and believed in their husbands and the vision God had given to Noah. They chose to stand firm with faith in God.

It is also worth noting that these three unnamed women were responsible for repopulating the whole earth after the flood.

5. LOT'S WIFE

Genesis 19:15-16,26 and Luke 17:30-32

A woman unnamed in the Bible, she was spared from the destruction of Sodom along with her husband and daughters. However, she failed to heed the Angel's simple instruction which was, "Don't look back." She looked back and was turned into a pillar of salt.

6. LOT'S DAUGHTERS

Genesis 19:4-38

L ot had two daughters, neither of whom are named in the Bible.

Their father offered them as sex slaves to the rampant men of Sodom who knocked on his door, wanting to defile the angels sent by God.

They later escaped with their father and ended up sequestered in a cave with him.

In order to secure the continuity of their lineage the girls decided to get their father drunk and take it in turns to sleep with him over the course of two days.

Both girls got pregnant and each gave birth to a son.

The older daughter birthed Moab, which meant 'from my father' (father of the Moabites), and the younger birthed Ben-Ammi which meant 'the son of my kin' (father of the Ammonites).

7. SARAH

Genesis 11-23 esp. Gen 20:12; 21:1-7

I nitially named Sarai, she was renamed Sarah, by God. Her name means princess. She was both half-sister and wife to Abraham.

The Bible describes her as extremely beautiful, so much so that Abraham, afraid that she would be taken from him, begged her to lie twice, saying she was his sister.

Although God had given Abraham a promise of a son, Sarah got tired of waiting and decided to assist God by offering her slave, Hagar, to Abraham as a wife to bear him a son. This decision resulted in numerous problems.

Sarah eventually gave birth to Isaac, the son of God's promise, at the age of ninety and subsequently died at one-hundred-and-twenty-seven.

8. HAGAR

Genesis 16 & 21

~

S arah's Egyptian slave, she is given to Abraham as a wife solely so he could bear children. When she became pregnant, pride crept in and she began to despise her mistress. Sarah responded by treating her harshly, so pregnant Hagar ran away.

Whilst in the desert she encountered an angel who told her to return home. The Angel told her she carried a son who would have greatness upon him, and she should name him Ishmael.

Fourteen years later, when Hagar's teenage son starts to mistreat Isaac, Sarah sends both Hagar and Ishmael away. In the desert, when they are both at the point of death, Hagar has another Angel encounter, and the pair are rescued by God.

9. REBEKAH

Genesis 24-28

The daughter-in-law and niece of Abraham and Sarah.

When Sarah died Isaac was distraught, so Abraham sent his trusted servant back to his hometown to find his son a wife. Rebekah was the woman, chosen by God for Isaac.

The Bible describes her as beautiful, so much so that Isaac tells the same lie as his father; he also claims she is his sister.

Barren for twenty-years, until God heard Isaac's prayers (Genesis 25:21), she became the mother of twin boys, Esau and Jacob.

She favours her younger son Jacob and is instrumental in him stealing his older brother's blessing. This led to so much strife between the brothers, it resulted in Jacob having to flee to Haran.

10. DEBORAH

Genesis 24; 35:8

Deborah is the nurse who accompanied Rebekah when she left her hometown in Aram for Canaan.

Many years later, the Bible records her journeying back to Canaan with Jacob and his family.

This suggests that at some point Deborah returned to Haran. Perhaps she was sent with Jacob when he fled from his brother's wrath.

We do know she died on the journey back to Canaan and was deeply mourned by Jacob and his household suggesting she was an important part of the family.

11. LEAH

Genesis 29-30; 35: 16-19; 37:3; 42:4

The first wife of Jacob, she attained this position through her father's deception. She was unloved by her husband, rejected and cast aside.

Only a few days after her marriage, her sister joined the household resulting in an intense battle for their husband's love and affection. Because she was unloved, God opened her womb and blessed her with numerous sons and one daughter.

She was also the mother of Judah; from whose line our salvation comes. When she died, she was buried with the Patriarchs of the family. (For a fictional and more detailed retelling of the life of Leah, please see my novel, *LEAH: Unnoticed. Unwanted. Unloved.*)

12. RACHEL

Genesis 29-31; 35

～

The second and favourite wife of Jacob; he worked fourteen years to secure her hand in marriage.

She was his chosen bride, but in an act of deception, her older sister Leah was given to Jacob instead. She joined the household seven days later and then made sure she withheld her husband from her sister.

She is described as extremely beautiful, just like her aunt Rebekah and great aunt Sarah. She was also a shepherdess like her aunt Rebekah, and I find it interesting that Jacob met Rachel at the well, just as Abraham's servant met Rebekah.

There were so many similarities between these women that I often wonder if Jacob saw his mother in Rachel.

Rachel was also barren for many years, until eventually she gave birth to Joseph. She died whilst giving birth to Benjamin, her second son and was buried by the roadside. (Read more about Rachel in my novel, *LEAH: Unnoticed. Unwanted. Unloved.*)

13. ZILPAH AND BILHAH

Genesis 29-35

These women were handmaids or slaves given to Leah and Rachel respectively as part of the wedding gifts from their father, Laban.

Both sisters gave their maids to Jacob as a wife, and each bore him two sons. Many years later, Bilhah ended up in bed with Leah's first son, Reuben.

14. DINAH

Genesis 34

Dinah, Jacob's only daughter, was born by Leah between the tenth and eleventh son. She was sadly raped by a Hivite Prince, Shechem. Her older brothers,

Simeon and Levi avenged her rape in a fascinating act of deception and murder.

Following this, she was rescued from the home of the man who raped her and we then hear nothing more about her life.

15. TAMAR

Genesis 38:6-30; Ruth 4:12; Matt 1:3

Chosen by Judah to be the wife of his firstborn son, Er, a wicked man who was subsequently killed. Left a widow, Tamar was given to Judah's second son, Onan, according to the culture of the day, so she could bear a child for her late husband.

Onan, knowing the child would not be his, deliberately spilt his seed and for this wickedness, he also died. Tamar was then sent home with a promise to wait for Judah's third son to be old enough to fulfil the custom and give her a son, but Judah had no intention of allowing this.

Many years later, Tamar disguised as a prostitute slept with Judah. When Judah heard of the pregnancy, he condemned her to death until she was able to prove that her unborn child was his. Tamar gave birth to twin boys Perez and Zerah, ancestors of Jesus.

16. POTIPHAR'S WIFE

Genesis 39: 1-20

Although unnamed in the Bible, Jewish history and the Torah considered her important enough to name her as Zulieka.

Married to Potiphar, the Captain of the King's Guard in Egypt, she lusted after the slave boy Joseph and made many attempts to seduce him without success.

Her last failed attempt left her so enraged and rejected that she lied to her husband saying that Joseph tried to rape her, holding as evidence his cloak which he abandoned when he fled from her seduction. This deception led to many years of imprisonment for Joseph.

17. ASENATH

Genesis 41:45, 50; 46:20

Named as the daughter of the priest Potiphera, she was an Egyptian woman who married Joseph. She had two sons with Joseph, Manasseh and Ephraim.

18. SHIPRAH AND PUAH

Exodus 1:15-21

These women were Hebrew midwives, ordered by Pharaoh to kill all male children born to the Hebrew women.

However, fearing the Lord they decided against doing such a wicked thing; instead, with boldness and courage, they lied to Pharaoh that the Hebrew women, unlike Egyptian women, had delivered quickly before they arrived.

Because of their faith and courage, God blessed both women with families of their own.

19. JOCHEBED

Exodus 2:1-10; 6:20; Numbers 26:59

Despite her name not often being remembered, Jochebed was, never-the-less, a woman of great faith, the wife of Amram, and the mother of Miriam, Aaron and Moses.

When she bore Moses, she saw that he was a special boy and hid him for three months during the time when Pharaoh wanted all male babies to be killed.

When he was too old to be hidden, she placed him in a well woven basket and strategically placed him in the river, praying that he would be saved.

Moses was found by Pharaoh's daughter, who later employed Jochebed as the wet nurse to feed him.

Only God could orchestrate something so remarkable, not only for Moses to be saved, but for his own mother to be paid to feed him.

Her story is testament to God's great plan and his love for his people.

20. MIRIAM

Exodus 1-2; 15:20-21. Numbers 20:1; 26:59

Miriam, the sister of Moses and Aaron, waited and watched over her baby brother in the river; she saw him picked up by Pharaoh's daughter, had the courage to approach her, and offered to get her a wet nurse. She then ran quickly to find her mother.

Growing up to become a prophet and worship-leader, she later criticised Moses and also his wife and as a consequence, ended up inflicted with leprosy. In an act of selfless love, Moses prayed to God on her behalf which resulted in her healing.

21. PHARAOH'S DAUGHTER

Exodus 2:5-10. Acts 7:21. Hebrews 11:24

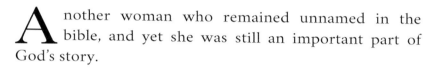

Another woman who remained unnamed in the bible, and yet she was still an important part of God's story.

Whilst we do not know much about her, we can assume that she was compassionate as she chose to raise a Hebrew baby who should have been condemned to death in accordance with her father's decree.

She was so invested in raising this boy that she was willing to pay for him to be fed and cared for.

22. ZIPPORAH

Exodus 2:15-22; 4:24-26; 18:2-6

The daughter of Jethro, the priest of Midian, she married Moses and bore him Gershom and Eliezer.

Moses had not circumcised his son and the Lord was going to kill him for his disobedience. Stepping in, Zipporah acted quickly to circumcise the boy saving Moses' life.

23. KOZBI ALSO KNOWN AS COZBI

Numbers 25:1-18

A Midianite woman who was brought into the Israelite camp by Zimri, son of Salu, the leader of the Simeonite family.

Zimri brought her at a time when God had passed judgement on the Israelite men who had been intermingling with Moabite women; they were to be executed as these women were idol worshippers.

This was a time of both chaos and sadness. Zimri chose this time to bring Kozbi to the camp, walking past Moses and the other men, into his tent; he then started to have sex with her.

Phinehas, the priest took a spear, walked into Zimri's tent, and drove it through Zimri right into Kozbi. She was a Midianite woman killed under a man.

24. THE DAUGHTERS OF ZELOPHEHAD

Numbers 26:33; 27:1-7. Joshua 17:3-7. 1 Chronicles 7:15

These five girls were named in the Bible as - Malhah, Noah, Hoglah, Milkah, and Tirzah. Their father, a descendent of Manasseh, son of Joseph, died in the desert before he received his share of the Promised Land.

These girls were so brave they approached Moses and other leaders and pleaded their case, asking, just because their father died with no sons should his name disappear? They asked for the share of their father's land amongst their relatives. This was counter cultural and had never been done before.

Moses then took their case before God and God found favour on their behalf. However, God doesn't stop there; He gives Moses firm directions on how to handle matters like this, moving forward.

Because of the bravery and courage of these girls, God declared that women now had a right of inheritance. The strict cultural laws of the day were changed on account of the bravery of these five girls.

25. RAHAB

*Joshua 26. Matthew 1:15. Hebrews 11:31. James
    2:25*

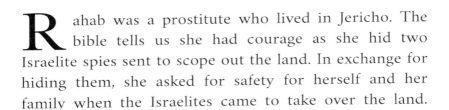

Rahab was a prostitute who lived in Jericho. The bible tells us she had courage as she hid two Israelite spies sent to scope out the land. In exchange for hiding them, she asked for safety for herself and her family when the Israelites came to take over the land. They agreed.

When the king came and enquired about the men, she lied to her king, telling him they had already left. She ultimately went with the Israelites after they invaded Jericho. She is named in the lineage of Jesus and is one of only two women named in Hebrews 11 as a woman of great faith. James described her as a righteous woman.

26. ACSAH

*Joshua 15:16-17. Judges 1:12-13. 1 Chronicles
    2:49*

Acsah was the daughter of Caleb, one of the spies who went to check out the promised land. Caleb offered his daughter as a prize to any man who could attack and kill their enemy, Kiriath Sepher.

Othniel, his nephew, rose to the challenge, killed the man, and received her as his prize-bride. She encouraged her husband to demand more and also asked her father for a special blessing of springs of water.

27. DEBORAH

Judges 4-5

∽

She is the second Deborah named in the Bible, married to Lappidoth. She was a Prophet and a Judge, the only female Judge in the Bible.

She gave a prophetic word to Barak, telling him God had assured him victory and he should raise an army and go and fight their enemy. Barak told her that he would only go if Deborah went with him.

She agreed to go to battle with him but told him that his reluctance to go alone would result in a woman taking the glory; the honour of killing the enemy leader would go to a woman.

28. JAEL

Judges 4:15-22; 5:24-27

Jael is the wife of Heber the Kenite and a woman of courage; she called out boldly to Sisera, the enemy-leader, and invited him into her tent, offered him comfort and pretended to care for him.

She gave him water and covered him, encouraging him to sleep while she watched out for his enemy.

When Sisera was fast asleep, she took a tent peg and killed him with it. She then called Barak to come and see the man that he had been looking for.

She was the woman who fulfilled Deborah's prophecy that a woman would take the glory for killing the enemy leader. Deborah immortalised Jael's courage and action with a song of celebration.

29. THE MOTHER OF JEPHTHAH

Judges 11:1-33

Another of the unnamed women of the Bible. She was a prostitute who birthed Jephthah. We don't know much about her other than that her son was cast aside and rejected from the family by the sons of his father's wives. They refused him an inheritance because he was the son of a prostitute.

Jephthah grew up to be a mighty warrior and the very people who rejected him, returned and pleaded with him to save them from their enemies. He eventually agreed to fight for them if they would make him their leader.

30. THE DAUGHTER OF JEPHTHAH

Judges 11:30-40

∽

Yet another woman who remains unnamed. We do know she was the only child of Jephthah the mighty warrior. After her father won the battle for the Lord, she came out excitedly to greet him with music and dancing.

However, before Jephthah went into battle, he made a vow to God that he would offer as a burnt sacrifice, the first thing that came out of his house on his return. He was moved to sorrow when this turned out to be his daughter and had to tell her of the promise he made to God.

This brave and courageous girl asked him to give her two months in the mountain with her friends, to grieve and weep for her virginity. When she returned two months later, Jephthah fulfilled his sorrowful vow to God.

31. THE MOTHER OF SAMSON

Judges 13:2-24

U nnamed, yet faithful, she was the wife of Manoah, a barren woman who longed for a child. God sent her a word with a promise that she would have a son.

However, God had certain instructions for her pregnancy – she must not drink wine or anything similar; she must not eat anything unclean; her son would be set apart from the womb, and upon his birth no razor should ever touch his head. He would be the chosen one deliver Israel from the Philistines.

This woman of faith took hold of the promise of God, obeyed the instructions, and gave birth to Samson.

32. DELILAH

Judges 16: 4-21

A Philistine woman, she came from a race declared as God's enemy.

Despite this, she became the object of Samson's affection, he loved her deeply and they developed a close relationship. Because of the access she had to Samson, the Philistine leaders offered her 5,500 pieces of silver to betray him.

They wanted to punish Samson as he had terrorised them and killed many Philistines; he remained undefeated due to his God-given strength.

Delilah was tasked with finding out the secret of his strength. Samson deceived her three times; each time she told the Philistines the wrong secret, they then tried to subdue Samson and failed.

Yet, she didn't give up; she was persistent in her desire to obtain the true secret and betray him. As a result, she bothered him day and night, almost to the point of death, until Samson, unable to deal with it any longer, told her the truth.

She successfully betrayed him resulting in Samson's capture and imprisonment.

33. NAOMI

Ruth 1-4

Married to Elimech, Naomi had two sons, Mahlon and Chilion. The family moved from Judah to Moab during a season of famine and settled there.

She was widowed and ten years later lost both sons. This left her with her two daughters-in-law, Ruth and Orpah.

When she heard that there was food in Judah, she decided to return home and encouraged her daughters-in-law to return to their own families due to the fact she had no more sons they could marry.

Bitter about her situation she claimed that God had dealt harshly with her; she changed her name from Naomi, which means pleasant, to Mara, which means bitterness.

Sometime later, she orchestrated the re-marriage of her daughter-in-law Ruth.

34. ORPAH

Ruth 1:4-16

A Moabite woman who was married to Naomi's son Chilion.

After the death of her husband, she was encouraged by her mother-in-law to return to her family, which she chose to do, and we hear nothing more about her.

35. RUTH

Ruth 1-4

Also a Moabite woman, Ruth was the wife of Naomi's son Mahlon.

After her husband died, Naomi encouraged her to go back home to her family, but she refused to leave Naomi and chose instead to journey with her to Judah.

She declared that Naomi's people would be her people and their God, her God. She faithfully cared for her mother-in-law, working long hours in a field to feed them both.

Boaz, the owner of the field, noticed her, and gave word that secured her food and protection. He had heard how kind she had been to her mother-in-law as her reputation for kindness had gone before her.

When she told Naomi, that Boaz had extended kindness to her, Naomi told her that Boaz could redeem her as his bride and gave her instructions on what she should do.

In an act of obedience, she embarked on a mission of humble seduction, offering herself to Boaz who gladly accepted and once a few cultural issues were dealt with, married her. She bore him one son Obed who was the grandfather of King David.

36. HANNAH

1 Samuel 1-2

O ne of Elkanah's two wives. She was deeply loved by her husband, even though she was barren. This resulted in her husband's other wife taunting her for many years, bringing her to the point of tears.

Elkanah assured her that his love for her did not waver despite her barrenness; he told her he was hurt that he was not enough for her, saying that he was worth more than ten sons. She, however, was desperate for children.

Then, one day, during the family's annual pilgrimage to Shiloh, Hannah was in the temple praying earnestly to God; she pleaded for a son, promising to dedicate him to God. Her prayer, accompanied by tears and silent mouthing of words, made her appear drunk to the priest, Eli.

When he challenged her, Hannah poured out her heart to him and, moved with compassion, Eli told her that God has heard. This resulted in the birth of Samuel.

After weaning the boy, she took him back to Eli to be in the service of God as she promised. She wrote the most beautiful prayer in 1 Samuel 2:1-11. God blessed Hannah with many more children.

37. PENINAH

1 Samuel 1

Peninah was Elkanah's second wife and Hannah's tormentor. As part of their family's annual pilgrimage to Shiloh, Elkanah would offer a sacrifice to God and the meat was then shared amongst the family: a portion was given to each woman and child.

Hannah would get only one portion, while Peninah would get a portion for herself and one portion for each of her children.

Because of this, she would taunt Hannah, making fun of her childlessness year after year. It is little wonder that when God finally blessed Hannah with children, she put a line or two in her prayer to God as a rebuke to Peninah.

38. MERAB

1 Samuel 14:49; 18:17-21. 2 Samuel 21:8

The oldest daughter of King Saul and used as a pawn in her father's plan to kill King David. Saul offered her as a reward to King David if he would go and fight a battle for him. Saul expected David to die in the battle, but instead David was victorious.

When David returned, Saul refused to keep his promise and instead gave Merab as a wife to Adriel with whom she had five sons.

39. MICHAL

1 Samuel 19:11-18; 25:44. 2 Samuel 3:13-14; 6:16-23. 1 Chronicles 15:29

Michal was King Saul's second daughter and deeply in love with King David. When her father heard this, he saw another opportunity. She was offered to David as a bride with his dowry being proof that he had killed 100 Philistines.

David killed 200 and presented evidence to Saul who was surprised; he had again assumed David would have been killed in battle.

After David married her and she uncovered a plot by her father to kill him; she warned her husband who fled, much to her father's displeasure. Saul then gave Michal to another man to marry.

Eventually, David recovered his wife, but things were no longer the same between them, maybe because by this time, he had married other wives.

She was sickened at David's excessive display of praise having recovered the Ark of God and scolded him. His response showed the discord between them.

She had no children.

40. ABIGAIL

1 Samuel 25; 27:2-4; 30:5. 1 Chronicles 3:1

∽

A sensible and beautiful woman, married to Nabal, a man the Bible describes as crude and mean; she described him as a fool.

She interceded for her husband's wickedness to King David, thus saving his life and the lives of all the men in her household.

When she told her husband how her quick thinking saved him, he had a stroke and died ten days later.

When David heard that Nabal was dead, he summoned and married Abigail. Much later, Abigail as well as all the families of David's men were captured.

This is another wife whom David eventually rescued and together, they had one son named Daniel.

41. THE MEDIUM OF EDNOR

1 Samuel 28:3-25

U nnamed and described as a medium. Mediums had been banned from using their evil powers by King Saul.At this time, King Saul had been rejected by God and Samuel the prophet was dead. Anxious and without direction, in desperation, he disguised himself and approached this medium, persuading her to use her evil powers to conjure up the spirit of Samuel.

She reluctantly agreed and called up Samuel. At that point she realises who was really in her house and she screamed. Samuel was not pleased to be disturbed and only had bad news for Saul. The medium of Ednor later encouraged Saul to eat. Preparing what could have been his last meal, he ate and left.

42. TAMAR (2)

2 Samuel 3:1-22

T he second Tamar named in the Bible, the daughter of King David, and the Bible describes her as beautiful. Her half-brother Amnon was so obsessed with her that he became ill from his longing for her.

His cousin and friend Jonadab, a crafty man, advised him to tell his father David that he was unwell and ask him to send his sister Tamar to come and care for him.

Tamar cooked his favourite meal and just before she served it to him, he sent all the servants away and requested she served him in his room.

When he started to seduce her, she begged him not to force himself on her, to instead ask their father to give her to him as a wife.

Her pleas fell on deaf ears and he raped her. His love then turned to hate resulting in him tossing her out of his house and locking the doors.

Distraught, she tore off her beautiful robe, worn only by the king's virgin daughters, put ashes on her head, and left, crying. David did not respond to this incident which infuriated Absalom her older brother. He took in his baby-sister and looked after her.

He then waited patiently for two years, until he could avenge his sister's rape by ordering the murder of Amnon.

43. RIZPAH

2 Samuel 3:7; 21:8- 14

Aiah's daughter and concubine of King Saul, to whom she bore two sons - Armoni and Mephibosheth. In a brutal act of revenge, both sons were murdered by hanging, along with the five sons of Merab, Saul's daughter.

After her sons were murdered, she was distraught and decided to keep vigil day and night, looking after their bodies, preventing any birds or wild animals from touching them; this continued for months despite the changing weather. When King David heard what she had done, he allowed their bodies, along with the retrieved bones of King Saul and Jonathan to be buried properly.

44. BATHSHEBA

2 Samuel 11-12. 1 Kings 1:11-31. Psalm 51.
Matthew 1:6

Bathsheba, one of the more well-known women in the bible, was the wife of Uriah, a loyal soldier to

King David. The bible notes her to have been a beautiful woman.

One day, while her husband was away in battle, King David, whilst on a rooftop, noticed her as she bathed. She was summoned by him and he slept with her. A few weeks later, she sent word that she was pregnant.

In desperation, David summoned her husband from battle and tried to get him to go home to his wife, hoping that he would sleep with her, thus passing the unborn child as being Uriah's. Loyal to the King and the other warriors in battle, Uriah refused to go home.

David requested that her husband be killed and after she mourned him, he married her but the son she bore died. God blessed her with another son, Solomon, who was loved by God and grew up to be a wise and wealthy king; he ultimately inherited the throne.

She is named in Matthew in the genealogy of Jesus.

45. THE WISE WOMAN FROM TEKOA

2 Samuel 14:1-20

Described as a wise woman, she was recruited by Joab to orchestrate the return of Absalom, King David's son. Joab instructed her on what to do and say, so she went to the King and pretended to be a widow with two sons, telling him that one son killed the other.

She beseeched the King to spare the life of the other son from the hands of the people who wanted him dead. David agreed to her request and informed her that her living son would be protected.

She then revealed her true request to the King, asking that he granted the same favour to his son, Absalom, whom he had banished for killing Amnon his half-brother who had raped Tamar.

David asked her if Joab had orchestrated this trick, and she says yes. David agreed to have Absalom returned, thanks to the input from this wise woman.

46. TAMAR (3)

2 Samuel 14:27

The third of the many Tamar's named in the Bible, she was the daughter of Absalom. All we know about her from the bible is that she is described as beautiful.

She was possibly named after her Aunty Tamar, who lived with them after she was raped.

47. ABISHAG

1 Kings 1:1-4; 2:13-25

Shunammite woman, young, beautiful, and a virgin girl given to King David when he was very old and could not keep warm. She became a human blanket, used to keep him warm, laying next to him, caring for him, waiting on him but remaining a virgin by his side.

After David died, one of David's sons, Solomon's older brother, Adonijah, spoke to Bathsheba to plead on his behalf to be given Abishag as a wife. Solomon however knew his true intentions — to usurp his throne and had him executed.

48. TWO PROSTITUTES

1 Kings 3:16-28

These women are both unnamed in the Bible but are described as prostitutes who lived together and had baby boys three days apart. They lived alone in the same household.

One night, one of the women fell asleep on her son and killed him. When she discovered what she had done, she swapped her dead son for the other woman's living son.

In the morning, the other woman recognised that the baby in her arms was not hers and an argument ensued. To settle the dispute, they went to King Solomon, each telling their side of the story.

Solomon, with great wisdom, then asked for a sword. He told both women that he would divide the baby and give each of them half. The real mother stopped the King and said he should give the baby to the other woman instead of killing him. The other woman said she wanted the baby divided into two.

Solomon, then recognising the truth handed the baby over to his mother, knowing that no mother would want her child dead.

49. THE QUEEN OF SHEBA

1 Kings 10: 1-13. 2 Chronicles 9: 1-12

Unnamed in the bible despite being a wealthy queen, she came from a land far away. Hearing about the wealth and wisdom of King Solomon, she decided to take a trip to visit him and test him with hard questions, arriving with a large caravan and many gifts.

Solomon answered all her questions, leaving her over-whelmed at his wisdom and also his great wealth. As well as leaving behind many gifts she took an equal amount with her when she returned to her own country.

50. THE WIVES AND CONCUBINES OF SOLOMON

1 Kings 11:1-13

The Bible records that King Solomon had 700 wives and 300 concubines. Many of his wives were foreigners who worshipped idols; women who were prohibited by God as wives, but Solomon did not listen.

His foreign wives eventually turned him away from worshipping only the one true God and he started to worship their idols as well, ultimately leading to his downfall.

51. JEZEBEL

1 Kings 16:31; 18:4-19; 19:1-2; 21:5-24. 2 Kings 9:7-37

A daughter of Ethbaal the king of the Zidonians, she was married to Ahab, one of the evilest kings that ever lived. She had three children, two boys, Ahaziah and Jehoram and a daughter Atlhaliah.

She was an unrepentant Baal worshipper, and she ordered the massacre of all of God's prophets whilst Elijah was away. Obadiah, one of the prophets hid 100 of them in two caves and fed them. Jezebel provided a sanctuary for 850 prophets of Baal and Asherah.

When Elijah returned, with a display of the power of the Almighty God who answers with fire, he killed all 850 prophets in one day.

When Jezebel heard this, she was furious and promised to kill Elijah within twenty-four hours causing him to flee. She also orchestrated the death of Naboth, a man who refused to sell his plot of land to King Ahab.

Jezebel died a gruesome death, as prophesied by Elijah. This involved being pushed out of a window, falling to her death, and her body eaten by hungry dogs.

52. THE WIDOW OF ZAREPHATH

1 Kings 17:7-24. Luke 4:24-26

Yet another unnamed woman in the Bible despite her great faith in God. A poor widow with one son, she was gathering sticks by the town's gate when she was approached by God's prophet, Elijah, who asked her for some food. She told him that she had only a little flour and oil left and the sticks she is gathering would be used to make their last meal before they died.

Elijah prophesied that her jar of flour and jug of oil would not run dry until the drought in their land ended. He asked her not to fear and to make him some bread to eat. She obeyed, cooked the bread and fed him, and the flour and oil never ran out.

Later on, her only son died whilst Elijah was with them. He resurrected the boy and gave him back to his mother.

Jesus talks about this woman in the book of Luke, telling his audience that God sent His prophet to a foreign widow.

53. THE WIDOW WITH THE MIRACLE OIL

2 Kings 4:1-7

Also unnamed, she had two sons and her husband died, leaving her in debt with no money to live on. When his creditors came to collect the money owed them and saw that she had none, they asked for her two sons as slaves as a repayment for the debt.

She hurried to the Prophet Elisha, begging him for help, and reminding him that her husband was also prophet in service to God.

Although the Bible does not go into much detail about her husband, Jewish history suggests that she was the widow of the prophet Obadiah, the one who hid 100 of God's prophets from Jezebel.

He spent all his money feeding them and also borrowed money from the household of Ahab to continue to feed them, which is probably why he died in debt.

Elisha asks the widow what she had in her house and she said a small jar of oil. He then told her to borrow as many jars as she could, ensuring she didn't just borrow a few.

Once she collected the jars, he told her to fill them up with the oil from her own small jar. This jar did not run out of oil until the last borrowed jar was filled to the brim.

The widow sold the oil and had enough money to pay off her debts and to live comfortably.

54. THE SHUNAMMITE WOMAN

2 Kings 4:8-37; 8:1-6

Described as a rich, compassionate woman who provided hospitality to the Prophet Elisha.

She cared for him so much that she asked her husband if they could build a permanent accommodation where the Prophet could stay whenever he visited. Her husband agreed and they built him a room on the roof of their house.

Elisha, moved by this woman's love and compassion, wanted to repay her. He asked her what he could do to help her, and she replied that she wanted nothing. Later, his servant Gehazi told him that the woman didn't have a son and her husband was much older.

Elisha called her and told her that within the year she would have a son. To her delight, a year later she gave birth to a son who she loved and adored.

One day, he took ill and died in her arms. Saying nothing, she took the boy, placed him on Elisha's bed in his upper room, and headed to meet Elisha in his hometown. She told him that her son was dead, and he sent his servant ahead of them with his staff to raise the boy.

The boy was only awakened when Elisha himself performed a miracle similar to that of Elijah when he raised the widow's son and the boy awakened.

Later, due to famine, she moved to the area where the Philistines lived, and remained there for seven years. When she returned home, she begged the King to restore her previously abandoned property and all is restored to her.

55. NAAMAN'S SERVANT

2 Kings 5:1-19

This young girl, captured from Israel, served as a slave to Naaman's wife. Knowing that her master had leprosy, she told her mistress about the Prophet Elisha in Samaria, confident that he could heal him.

Naaman's wife encouraged her husband to go to see Elisha and he eventually gets healed after he humbled himself and listened to Elisha's instructions. This was all thanks to the courage of this unnamed slave girl.

56. TWO STARVING WOMEN

2 Kings 6:24-31; 7:1-16

Unnamed in the Bible, they lived at a time of severe famine in Samaria. Starving, they both agreed to eat their sons to survive — one woman's son the first day, then the other woman's the next day.

However, on the second day the other woman hid her son and refused to bring him out to be killed and eaten. The case was brought before the King who in distress was moved to tears and tore his robe, dismayed at what his kingdom had become.

The sad part of this story was that just the next day, the land was filled with much food and an abundance of wealth, left by the fleeing Arameans.

57. ATHALIAH

2 Kings 11. 2 Chronicles 22-23

The daughter of Jezebel and Ahab, she gave bad advice to her son, Ahaziah, who was a King and he ended up assassinated. Following the assassination, she ascended to the throne and declared herself Queen.

To be certain no one would usurp her she ordered the murder of every single member of the royal family including her own grandchildren.

However, baby Joash was rescued by his aunt and hidden for seven years, eventually being crowned king much to Athaliah's shock and anger. The priests who crowned Joash as king ordered Athaliah to be killed.

58. JEHOSHEBA

2 Kings 11:2. 2 Chronicles 22:11

Jehosheba was the woman who rescued her nephew Joash from the death ordered by Athaliah, his wicked grandmother, despite great personal risk. She hid him and his nurse in the temple for seven years, thus playing a decisive role in the protection of one of the rightful heirs to the throne.

59. GOMER

Hosea 1:3; 14:4

Despite her being a prostitute, God instructed his servant Hosea to marry her. They had one son together, yet Gomer kept running back to her old life as a prostitute.

Their marriage was an analogy of God's relationship with the Israelites, who kept running to serve false gods. Hosea kept running after his wife and bringing her back; she had two more children whom he suspected were not his.

God told him how to name these children – the girl was to be named Lo-Ruhamah which means 'not loved' and the boy Lo- Amni which means 'Not my people'. Gomer ran away again, and God told Hosea to go after her; this time she was living with another man.

Hosea had to buy back his wife for 15 Shekels of silver and barley. God told Hosea to love her the same way he loved the Israelites.

60. NOADIAH

Nehemiah 6:14

Named as a prophet, she, and the other prophets, were accused of intimidation by Nehemiah. Though his main adversaries were Tobiah and Sanballat, Noadiah was also named by Nehemiah as one of his tormentors in his prayer to God.

61. QUEEN VASHTI

Esther 1:7-20

The wife of the Persian King Xerxes. During an elaborate, seven-day, alcohol-filled banquet thrown by the king, she was summoned by him to come and dance before his drunken guests. She was ordered to wear her crown (maybe only her crown, the Bible is not clear) to display her beauty. Queen Vashti also held her own banquet for the women in the palace.

When she was summoned, she refused to appear before the king and, as a consequence, was banned from ever seeing the king again; she was also dethroned and banished to the harem. This was done as a warning to the women of the land so they would not think about disobeying their husbands.

62. QUEEN ESTHER

Esther 2-9

A Jewish orphan, adopted by her uncle and raised in the ways of the Lord. One of the many beautiful virgins taken into the King's Harem to be prepared for a night with King Xerxes in order for him to choose a suitable replacement for Queen Vashti.

She was liked and favoured by the King's Eunuch and listened to his advice, carrying herself with dignity during the session of preparation. When she had her night with the King, she was chosen as the next Queen.

Later, she was informed of a plot within the palace to kill all Jews. Her uncle sent word that she should approach the King and beg for mercy for her people.

She initially responded, "No," out of fear until her uncle, Mordecai, reminded her that she would die alongside the other Jews and that she may have been placed in the palace 'for such a time as this'.

In an act of bravery, after calling for all Jews to three days of fasting and prayer, Queen Esther broke cultural and national protocol, risking her immediate execution by approaching the King uninvited.

The King spared his beautiful bride and agreed to honour her invitation for dinner. She eventually told him of the plot to kill her people which led to the execution of the perpetrator and the saving of the Jewish people.

63. ZERESH

Esther 5:9-14; 6:12-14

Wife to Hamman, the man who plotted to kill all Jews. As a foreigner, his people had previously been killed by Jews and the disobedience of Mordecai (Esther's uncle), who was unwilling to bow down to him, annoyed him greatly.

Zeresh encouraged her husband to build a seventy-five-foot pole which he would use to impale Mordecai once the decree to have all Jews killed had been sanctioned.

When Hamman's wicked plan was uncovered this was the pole used to impale her husband.

64. JOB'S WIFE

Job 2:9-10

Another woman unnamed in the Bible. She was married to Job, a righteous man in the eyes of God and they had ten children — seven sons and three daughters.

Job was a very wealthy man with lots of servants, land, and other possessions. When God allowed Job to be tested by the devil, her ten children were killed, and all her husband's possessions were gone. He was left sick and in pain.

Heartbroken she encouraged Job to curse God and die.

Despite this, Job maintained his integrity and refused to speak against God. God restored to Job a double portion of all that was lost and blessed him with another ten children - seven boys and three girls in honour of his previous children.

65. JOB'S DAUGHTERS

Job 42:13-15

When Job's fortune was restored, God blessed him with three daughters who are named as Jemimah, Keziah and Keren-Happuch.

The Bible described them as the most beautiful girls in all the land. It is interesting to note that his sons are not named but his daughters are named.

Job went against the conventional practice of his time; in a counter cultural move, he gave his three daughters an inheritance like his sons.

PART TWO

WOMEN IN THE NEW TESTAMENT

Matthew - Revelation

1. ELIZABETH

Luke 1:5-60

A descendant of Aaron and married to the Priest Zechariah. The Bible describes them as righteous people. She was barren and well along in years; yet the Angel Gabriel appeared to Zechariah and told him they would have a son and they were to call him John.

Elizabeth was joyful at the news; she said God had taken away her disgrace and when she became pregnant, she remained secluded for five months.

She was visited by her cousin Mary and was filled with the Holy Spirit. At the sound of Mary's voice, the baby in Elizabeth's womb leapt for joy and she began to prophesy.

2. MARY

Matthew 1:18 – 2:11. Luke 1:26 – 38; 2:1 – 51.
Acts 1:14

Mary, possibly the most well-known of the women in the bible, was a young virgin girl engaged to be married to Joseph, a descendant of David. She found favour with God and was chosen to be the one to give birth to Jesus the Messiah.

She received a word from an Angel sent by God who told her she would conceive and give birth to a son. She asked him how this could happen as she is a virgin and he replied that the Holy Spirit would come upon her.

The Angel also told her that her cousin Elizabeth, the one whom they called barren, was six months pregnant even at her advanced age.

Mary didn't argue; she didn't worry about Joseph or what this prophecy would mean for her marriage; she didn't worry about her reputation; she just willingly chose to serve and declared, 'I am the Lord's servant, may your word to me be fulfilled'.

She immediately visited Elizabeth and discovers that she is, indeed, pregnant. Even though Joseph wanted to quietly break off his engagement to her, an Angel appeared to him and told him not to be afraid to take Mary as his wife.

Mary gave birth to Jesus in a manger, raised him, encouraged him to perform his first recorded miracle — turning water into wine – and was by his side when He was crucified.

3. ANNA

Luke 2:36 - 38

The daughter of Penuel, she married and was widowed after just seven years. She was a prophet who took up residence in God's temple, dedicating the rest of her life to worshipping Him day and night; she never left.

She was there when Mary and Joseph brought baby Jesus to be consecrated, gave thanks for witnessing a special moment, and prophesied over Jesus.

4. HERODIAS

Matthew 14:3 – 14. Mark 6:17 – 28. Luke 3:19 – 20

Initially married to Phillip, she left him and married his brother Herod. She took offence and held a grudge against John the Baptist who confronted Herod, telling him it was unlawful for him to take her as his wife.

When her daughter, in the opportunity of a lifetime, danced well for Herod and was offered anything she wanted, Herodias told her to request the head of John the Baptist on a platter.

Herod, unable to renege on his oath, ordered the execution of John the Baptist and his head was given to Herodias.

5. HERODIAS' DAUGHTER

Matthew 14:6 – 14. Mark 6:21 – 28

Another who remains unnamed in the Bible, she was a talented dancer and performed beautifully at a feast in honour of Herod's birthday.

He was so pleased with her performance he promised with an oath that she could receive anything she wanted.

Like any young girl would, she ran to her mother, filled with excitement, possibly thinking of all the great things she could request.

Sadly, her mother used her blessing as a pawn in a revenge game and asked her to ignore every other desire she could have dared to hope for, but to instead ask for the head of John the Baptist as her reward.

6. PETER'S MOTHER-IN-LAW

Matthew 8:14 – 15

U nnamed in the Bible, she lived with Peter and his wife and was in bed with a fever. When Jesus came to visit and saw that she was unwell, He touched her hand and healed her. She immediately got up, made a meal, and served Him.

7. THE WIDOW FROM NAIN

Luke 7:11 – 17

N ot named in the Bible but a woman who had her fair share of sorrow: first, her husband died leaving her a widow; then, her only son died as well. Wailing alongside a large crowd as part of the procession to bury her son, she was in great distress, filled with much sorrow, openly weeping, and in deep mourning.

Jesus saw her and was moved with deep compassion telling her not to cry. He interrupted the procession, touched the coffin and told the young man to get up; the dead son woke up, started talking, and was restored to his mother.

8. THE BLEEDING WOMAN

Mark 5:25 – 34. Luke 8:43 – 48. Matthew 9: 20-22

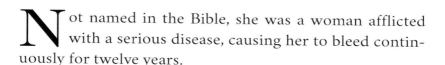

N ot named in the Bible, she was a woman afflicted with a serious disease, causing her to bleed continuously for twelve years.

Because of her bleeding, she was classed as unclean and cut off from society resulting in her spending all her money on doctors and various cures. It was to no avail as, instead of getting better she was getting worse.

She heard about Jesus and in desperation, took a bold step of faith; she ignored the cultural norms, hid in the crowd, possibly crawling, until she was just close enough to grab hold of the hem of Jesus' garment. With just one touch she was immediately healed.

Jesus felt power leave Him and asked who touched Him. She owned up and Jesus called her **daughter**. He affirmed her faith, declared her healed, and sent her away in peace.

9. THE CRIPPLED WOMAN

Luke 13:10 – 17

Another woman unnamed in the Bible, she had been crippled by an evil spirit for eighteen years, bent over and unable to fully stand. One Sabbath day, she was at the Synagogue listening to Jesus teaching.

When he saw her, called her over, and healed her. She immediately stood straight and began to praise God. The Synagogue leaders were not pleased; they said that there were six days for work and that is when people should come to be healed.

Jesus humiliated them by calling them hypocrites and challenged them by asking which of them would not tend to their animals on the Sabbath? How much more a daughter of Abraham who needed to be set free.

10. THE POOR WIDOW

Mark 12:41 – 44. Luke 21:1 – 4

Unnamed in the Bible, known only as a poor widow who worshipped in the Temple, she followed a procession of people going to put money in the Temple treasury. When her turn came, she placed two small copper coins, giving all she had. Jesus, who was with His disciples, watched her from a distance.

He told them that the poor widow had given much more than the others. He said the others gave out of their abundance, but she gave everything she had. He taught His disciples that her sacrifice was more valuable.

11. THE CANAANITE/SYROPHOENICIAN WOMAN

Matthew 15:21 – 28, Mark 7:24 – 30

This lady is another of the many unnamed woman in the Bible. The Gospel of Mark tells us she was Greek, born in Syrian Phoenicia; the Gospel of Matthew describes her as a Canaanite woman. She was a foreigner and non-Jew, and her daughter was possessed by a demon.

On hearing that Jesus was in a house nearby she rushed to him, falling at His feet, and begging Him to heal her daughter. Jesus told her that He came for the Jews and it was not right to give the bread meant for the children to the dogs.

The woman, persistent and focused on her mission, told Jesus that even the dogs eat the crumbs from the master's table. Jesus responded to her faith and healed her daughter.

12. THE ADULTEROUS WOMAN

John 8:1 – 11

Caught in the 'very act' of adultery, this unnamed woman was humiliated and dragged into the middle of the Temple courts where Jesus was teaching by some Scribes and Pharisees who wanted to use her to trap Jesus with the law.

They told Jesus that according to the law of Moses, the woman should be stoned to death. Jesus did not respond to them; instead, He bent down and started to write on the ground with his finger.

They kept questioning Him, pushing for a response, so He got up and told them that whoever, among them is without sin should cast the first stone. He stooped down again and continued to write on the ground.

Convicted, they all left one after the other starting with the oldest ones, until none of her accusers were left. Jesus, the only one truly able to cast the first stone offered her mercy; He told her to go and sin no more.

13. MARY MAGDALENE

Matthew 27:55- 28:10. Luke 8:1-3; 24:1-10.
John 19:25; 20: 1-18

The second Mary named in the New Testament and also called Magdalene. She was a woman healed by Jesus when he cast out seven demons.

She then dedicated herself to supporting His ministry with her own money. She stood by Jesus from the time of His arrest to His crucifixion.

The Gospel of John records Mary standing outside Jesus's empty tomb on resurrection day crying. She told the Angels who asked why she was crying that they have taken her Lord away and she doesn't know where.

Jesus then appeared to her, but she didn't immediately recognise Him until He called her name. In her excitement she rushed to touch Him, but He told her not to as He has not yet ascended.

Jesus told her to go and tell the others that He has risen making Her the first evangelist, spreading the good news.

14. MARTHA

Luke 10:38– 42. John 11:5-44; 12:2-7

A woman who loved, and was loved by, Jesus. She had two siblings, Mary and Lazarus, and owned her own home where she often welcomed Jesus and His disciples.

On one occasion, she was busy preparing a meal for them when she noticed her sister sitting at the feet of Jesus; she was annoyed and went to Jesus, telling Him to tell Mary to help her.

Jesus told Martha that only one thing is needed and that is Him. He told her she was worried and upset about too many things that she should instead focus only on Him. He also said that Mary had made the right choice and He would not take that away from her.

15. MARY (MARTHA'S SISTER)

Luke 10:38 – 42. John 12:2-7

The third Mary in the New Testament: a woman who dearly loved Jesus, she sat at Jesus' feet while her sister was busy cooking and clearly flustered by the busyness of cooking for so many guests. Yet, Mary's focus remained on Jesus.

In another story, Jesus was being honoured as a guest and a meal was prepared and served to him. Martha was busy cooking and serving, with Mary once again at Jesus' feet, this time not just sitting down and listening to Him: she took twelve ounces of expensive perfume, poured it over Jesus' feet and wiped it with her hair, to Judas's disapproval.

Mary was criticised twice, once by her sister, the other by a disciple. Both times she sat at the feet of Jesus; both times, Jesus defended her.

N.B. – There are many Bible scholars who suggest Mary of Bethany is the same as Mary Magdalene. The Bible has not made this clear so I have separated them in this book.

16. THE WOMAN FROM SAMARIA, AT THE WELL

John 4:5-42

Unnamed in the Bible but described by her ethnicity. The conversation she had with Jesus at the well is the longest recorded conversation between Jesus and any woman in the Bible.

Jesus asked this woman to give Him water, much to her dismay, because Jews and Samaritans didn't mix. Jesus offered this woman living water which she so desperately wanted.

When Jesus told her to go and call her husband, she responded with the truth — she had no husband. Jesus then told her about her life; she was a woman who had already had five husbands and was living with a man to whom she is not married.

Without responding, she entered into a religious conversation with Him about the place of worship. Jesus then revealed Himself to her as the Messiah. When the disciples returned, they were astonished to see Jesus talking to her.

She left them and rushed into her hometown and told them about Jesus. Many people believed in Jesus because of her testimony.

17. PILATE'S WIFE

Matthew 27:11-26

Another unnamed woman of the bible, yet one of great faith, she was there when Jesus was brought before Pilate for judgement.

During this process, she sent a message to Pilate, telling him not to get involved with Jesus' death. She told him

that Jesus was an innocent man and that she had a trou-
bling dream about Him.

18. SALOME

Mark 15:40-41; 16:1. Luke 8:3

A follower of Jesus; one of the women who supported His ministry. She was among the women who watched from a distance as Jesus was cruci-fied. She went with a few women to buy spices to anoint the body of Jesus.

19. MARY (MOTHER OF JAMES AND JOSEPH)

Matthew 27:55-56. Mark 15:40-41; 16:1. Luke 24:1-11

The fourth Mary found in the New Testament; she is the mother of James and Joseph, and recognised as one of the women who loved Jesus and supported His ministry.

20. THE MOTHER OF ZEBEDEE'S SONS

Matthew 20:20-28; 27:55-56

Although unnamed in the Bible, she was a passionate mother who made a bold and audacious request. She knelt before Jesus with a request — grant that my sons will sit one on the right and one on the left in your kingdom.

Jesus asked her if they could endure what was set before him and both boys responded saying they could. Jesus told them that they would indeed drink of His cup, but the decision of who sits on his left or right is for God to make not Him. When the other disciples heard what happened, they are dismayed. Jesus used it as a teaching opportunity, telling them that whoever desires greatness must be willing to be a servant.

21. JOANNA

Luke 8:2-3; 24:1-11

The wife of Chuza, Herod's steward, and one of the women that Jesus heals of evil spirits and infirmities. She is another of the women mentioned in the bible who supported Jesus' ministry financially. There is only one mention of her, in the Gospel of Luke, and she is amongst the women who went to embalm Jesus not knowing He had risen.

22. SUSANNA

Luke 8:2-3

Mentioned only once, in the Gospel of Luke, she was a woman delivered from spirits by Jesus. She became a follower of Jesus and also supported His ministry financially.

23. MARY (CLOPAS' WIFE)

John 19:25

The fifth Mary mentioned in the New Testament and married to Clopas. We know she stood near the cross as Jesus was crucified.

24. JESUS' AUNT

John 19:25

Although unnamed, the bible tells us she was Mary's (the Mother of Jesus) sister. She was beside Mary at the crucifixion of Jesus, supporting her sister through what must have been a grim time.

25. SAPPHIRA

Acts 5:1-11

The wife of Ananias; the couple lived in community with other followers of Jesus. They sold a piece of land and she agreed with her husband to keep for themselves some of the proceeds of the sale and lie about it.

This happened at a time when everyone in the community had decided to live as one, pooling together all their resources and sharing them so no one was left without. Ananias gave the rest of the proceeds of the sale to Peter, claiming that it was the total amount.

When Peter confronted him, he lied about it and died for his deception. This was unknown to Sapphira, who arrived hours later and told the same lie.

Disappointed, Peter told her that because she conspired with her husband to lie to God, the men who had just buried her husband would take her as well, thus her deception led to her death.

26. TABITHA (DORCAS)

Acts 9:36-42

Named Tabitha, her Greek name was Dorcas. The Bible described her as a woman who was always doing good. When she became ill and died, her body was washed, kept in a room upstairs and prepared for burial.

Some disciples of Jesus heard that Peter was in a nearby town, so they sent two men to ask him to come at once. Peter arrived to meet numerous crying widows, mourning for a woman who had been so wonderful to them; they showed Peter the evidence of her greatness, the clothes she had made for them.

Peter prayed for Dorcas, Jesus resurrected her, and Peter returned Dorcas, well and alive to the people who loved her dearly.

27. MARY (MOTHER OF JOHN MARK)

Acts 12:12-16

The seventh Mary mentioned in the New Testament, mother of John who was also called Mark.

She was noted for opening her home to the disciples and followers of Jesus who gathered to pray for Peter who had been arrested, doing so at great personal risk, at a time when people had been banned from following Jesus.

28. RHODA

Acts 12:12-16

A servant in Mary's (the mother of John Mark) house who was with them while they were praying for Peter. When she heard a knock on the door, she ran quickly to see who it was, careful not to open it and let the authorities in.

She heard Peter's voice; in her excitement, she left him standing outside and rushed to tell the disciples that Peter was at the door.

They told her she must be dreaming, for they said Peter was in prison. She insisted. More knocks were heard so the disciples open the door to find, Rhoda was right, it was Peter!

29. LYDIA

Acts 16:14-40

She was a businesswoman from Thyatira, who sold expensive purple fabric. She believed in God but when she overheard Paul teaching about Jesus, she believed in Jesus in addition to God, resulting in her ensuring that she and her entire household were baptised.

Lydia welcomed Paul and his followers into her home, providing food and shelter for them. Later, Paul and Silas were imprisoned and when they were released, they returned to her house where they met with other believers.

She was a woman willing to further the gospel of Jesus, allowing her home to be a gathering place for a faith for which many were being imprisoned.

30. THE FORTUNE TELLER

Acts 16:16-19

~

U nnamed in the Bible, we know she was a slave girl possessed with a spirit of divination. Her masters used her to make a lot of money as the spirit within her made her a fortune teller. She saw Paul and Silas and recognised them as men of God.

She followed them around for many days, crying with a loud voice that they are indeed men of God. After this goes on for some days, Paul, annoyed, rebuked the spirit within her in Jesus' name.

That very hour, the girl was delivered from the evil spirit, much to her owners' anger as their source of wealth had gone. Her masters seized Paul and Silas, dragged them before the courts, and they ended up in prison.

31. EUNICE

Acts 16:1. 2 Timothy 1:5

~

E unice, although a Jewish woman, believed in Jesus. She was married to a Greek man and was the mother of Timothy. Her own mother, Lois, is described as a woman of great faith which she passed on to Eunice, who in turn passed it on to her son Timothy. Timothy became the Apostle Paul's protégé, growing in faith and in turn helping others grow.

32. PAUL'S SISTER

Acts 23:16

A nother woman unnamed in the Bible. It was her son who uncovered the plot to kill his uncle Paul; the brave young boy told Paul what he heard thus saving his life. Without Paul's nephew, his ministry may have been cut short.

Even though we don't hear much about this woman, we can assume that they were a close-knit family and she raised her son with the right values, giving him the courage to speak up and save his uncle's life.

33. DRUSILLA

Acts 24:24-27

A Jewish woman; all we know about her is that she was the wife of Governor Felix.

34. BERNICE

Acts 25:13.&23; 26:30

Mentioned three times in the Bible, each time in the company of King Agrippa. She was involved in determining the fate of Paul, agreeing with the others concerned that Paul had done nothing deserving of death.

The Bible is silent on her relationship with King Agrippa but Roman history suggests that they were siblings and she was involved in an incestuous relationship with her brother.

35. PRISCILLA

Acts 18:1-26. Romans 16:3-4. 1 Corinthians 16:19. 2 Timothy 4:19

The wife of Aquila, together they had a tent-making business: a common interest that they shared with Paul. They joined him as missionaries, and he left them in Ephesus where they continued to preach and teach the gospel.

Paul recognised this couple as people who risked their lives for him; he described them as co-workers in Jesus and they later started a church in their own home.

36. PHILIP'S DAUGHTERS

Acts 21:8-9

These four girls were the daughters of Phillip the Evangelist. They are all unnamed in the Bible, spoken only of as unmarried girls blessed with the gift of Prophecy.

37. PHOEBE

Romans 16:1-2

A Deacon in the church of Cenchreae, she was affirmed by Paul who sent her to Rome as a missionary. He asked the church he sent her to, to welcome her, receive her well and help her. Paul confirmed that she had been of great help to him and many others.

38. TYRPHENA, TRYPHOSA, AND PERSIS

Romans 16:12

Three women who Paul acknowledged as 'women who work hard for the Lord'; he sent greetings to them in his letter to a church in Rome, indicating that they were important to him.

39. RUFUS'S MOTHER

Romans 16:13

Unnamed in the Bible other than as the mother of Rufus. Paul described her as a woman who had been a mother to him as well.

40. JULIA AND THE SISTER OF NEREUS

Romans 16:15

As Paul concluded his letter to the Church in Rome, he sent his greetings to these women among a list of people he mentions. No one knows why Paul affirmed these women but they must have been important to him to be included in his letter.

41. PETER'S WIFE

1 Corinthians 9:5

U nnamed in the Bible, we know little about her. The Bible tells us that Jesus healed her mother. When Paul wrote to the churches in Corinth, he told them that Peter travelled with his wife and described her as a believing wife.

42. CHLOE

1 Corinthians 1:11-13

A woman whom Paul mentions in the Bible, although the details were not directly about her, but about members of her household who told him that there were disagreements in the church.

They quarrelled about who to follow; some say they followed Paul, some Apollos, some Peter, and some Jesus.

When Paul was informed of this, he corrected them, emphasising that there was no division in Christ Jesus.

43. NYMPHA

Colossians 4:15

W hen Paul wrote to the Church in Colossae he sent his greeting to Nympha and the church that met at her house.

44. EUODIA AND SYNTYCHE

Philippians 4:2-3

P aul recognised these women as followers of Jesus. These were women who had been at his side as co-workers, working hard to further the Gospel of Jesus.

However, there was an issue between the women, and they were unable to agree. Paul pled with them to be of the same mind in Christ and to settle the disagreements between them because they both belonged to the Lord.

45. THE CHOSEN LADY

2 John 1

J ohn wrote a beautiful letter to this unnamed woman in the Bible, and her children. He described her as the chosen lady whom he loved in truth; everyone else who knew the truth loved her as well. It was a beautiful letter to this woman.

46. JEZEBEL

Revelation 2:18-29

T he second Jezebel mentioned in the Bible, she was just as bad as the first. She was a false prophet who misled some of the people in the church in Thyatira. She led them into sexual immorality and eating the foods sacrificed to idols.

She was unrepentant and yet was tolerated by the church and allowed to exist amongst them. A prophetic letter to the church warned them about the woman, describing her fate in detail, the fate that would be shared by those who continued to follow her without repentance.

PART THREE

THE LIAR

A Short Story
Genesis 37:12-28 & Genesis 39

Desperately clinging to his cloak, fresh tears roll down already soaked cheeks as rage rumbles in her stomach; it reminds her of the unsatisfied hunger ravaging within her soul. The desire for the man who narrowly escaped her grasp cuts deep into her very being, leaving her bare and exposed.

Rocking back and forth on the vast expanse of the empty bed, her eyes squint slightly and she rubs her temples impulsively. How could he resist her again? Her mind runs into a thousand different directions, after all she has done, after twelve months of longing for him, she thought today was the day she would break him. The stars had said so and she knew she read them correctly.

Zuleika, wife to one of the most influential men in Egypt, stares at her reflection in the mirror. She is beautiful; every fibre of her being knows this to be true. Her beauty is lauded throughout Egypt. An Egyptian goddess in her own right, her skin although a light shade of brown, looks like a shade closer to golden olive, is rich, soft and blemish free. Her hair is darker than midnight: long and straight all the way down to her waist: thick and full just like her lips.

Although she is slender, her body curves subtly in just the right places to entice any man. But not the man she hungers for deep in her soul, not the man who has just wrenched himself from her grasp and run away. She punishes herself by pulling his cloak to her nose, drinking in the fragrance of him. A combination of sweet, scented oils and his sweat, it leaves her feeling intoxicated and she gasps for air.

The loud bang of the front door jolts her back into the present moment and the realisation sinks in deeper. Joseph has fled; he has left her lying in bed, naked and alone, covered only in her bitter shame.

Her nostrils flare viciously, and nasal liquid drips unfettered into her partially opened lips, giving her a taste of the disappointment she suffers. She sits up, still trembling, drags her unwilling legs out of the bed and stands up. Walking towards the large glass window, she looks out in time to see the back of his hair as he runs towards the servant quarters.

Zuleika places her right hand on the window as though she can touch him and places her left hand on her heart as though trying to keep him from running away with it, or at least contain the pain she feels. After staring at the empty courtyard for a few minutes, she stumbles back, her mind racing and her heart pounding as though fighting to leave her chest. She looks back towards the bed, at the space on the floor, where his cloak now lies where it was tossed on the floor at her feet.

She stares at it for a few moments and then turns to look at the window again, her gaze fixed on the exact place she saw his head before he turned towards the slave quarters and she lost sight of him. She whispers gently, "Joseph," and pauses, as though conjuring up his image before her. Standing straighter, again she calls his name, this time louder, firmer, and with venom, "You will pay for this disrespect with your life".

Zuleika picks up the cloak from the floor and strides back to her bed, sits on the rug and places the cloak on the floor beside her. There is no one else in the house but in just a few moments, the household will return from the festival, the one she excused herself from attending a few short hours before.

As she waits for the household to return, so she can enact her plan, her mind wanders back to twelve months ago, to when this all began.

Twelve Months Previously

Joseph walks the short distance from his small room in the slave quarters, through the large courtyard and into the main house. He had been summoned by Potiphar. His hands perspired slightly, a sign of his anxiety. What could Potiphar want from him, this early in the day?

His master had been gone for over a week, attending to matters of the state. He wasn't just an officer of Pharaoh; he was the captain of the Guard; this meant a huge responsibility lay on his shoulders as well as him having to be away from his house for many days at a time.

As Joseph walks, he slows his steps, forcing his mind to run through the events of the last week. As hard as he tried, he could not remember anything that had occurred that was a reason to be summoned before dawn.

He knew that he had done everything that was required of him and he had chosen to do much more including counting all the grain bags and accounting for the live-stock. He had also personally hand sewn missing stiches on Potiphar's garments and attended to the sick horses in Potiphar's stables, using herbs he walked hours to find.

Joseph stands in front of his master's door as he wipes his palms, slick with sweat, vigorously on his shirt. He pauses briefly and murmurs a prayer. "Lord, please go before me, your servant is to stand in front of a master who commands my ways, but you oh Lord command my life. Please give me favour before him and be with me as you have been with me all the days of my life"

Before he raises his hand to knock, Potiphar opens the door.

"Joseph, come in, I heard you outside the door whispering, is all well with you?"

Joseph walks in and bows his head before his master. "It is well with me my master" he responds and takes the seat that Potiphar offers.

Potiphar strolls towards the long wooden table at the back of the room and pours himself a glass of strong wine. Although early in the morning, he had been up most of the night unable to sleep.

"I can tell that you are concerned Joseph, you need not be. I know the sun is yet to rise and these early mornings are for resting eyes, but I have some things I urgently need to discuss with you before I am set to leave again in a few hours. I will be gone for a few days." He shakes his glass of wine, as though explaining to Joseph the reason he is drinking so early in the morning.

The room is large and tastefully furnished with both Egyptian and foreign pieces. A small lamp fills the room with the only light. Potiphar drinks deeply and starts pacing around the room, pausing only briefly to sip. There is a moment of continued silence while Joseph sits and waits.

Potiphar looks keenly at this young man he bought from Ishmaelite's traders many years ago. He was amongst many slaves that the traders brought for sale and barely Eighteen years old at the time.

From the first time Potiphar saw Joseph, he took an immediate liking to the young Hebrew man. There was strength in his eyes, even though his body was covered in wounds and lacked flesh, a tell-tale sign that the travelling traders gave the slaves little or no food to eat.

Potiphar quickly bought him, paying more than he would have for any other slave – twenty shekels of Silver – after hard bargaining from the forty shekels the Ishmaelite's had initially asked for.

Hebrew boys were hard workers they insisted, and when he hesitated, they offered him another slave, older and bigger than Joseph for only twenty shekels of silver. Potiphar insisted on buying Joseph and over the years, it seemed a worthwhile investment.

Potiphar watched with such joy, each year as his household prospered. Everything he put in Joseph's command multiplied. It was clear Joseph was blessed by his God and the blessing was extended to Potiphar's house.

Although it is only a few minutes, it feels like many hours until Potiphar finally speaks. He paces up and down the room as he says, "Joseph, I have watched you work hard these last few years. Everything I give you to do, you do without fault. It is clear to see that your God is with you and he causes your hand to prosper. I see it, I see with my own eyes the work of your hands and it is good. There-fore, today, I want to put everything I own into your hands, into your care. Today, I want to make you the master of all slaves and the overseer of my house. Every-thing in my household today, I put under your authority"

Potiphar stops pacing and walks towards Joseph, the sun now rising slowly behind him pouring natural light into the room. He stares directly at Joseph, "Are you able young man?" he asks.

Joseph bows his head before Potiphar, courage from the Lord fills his bones and he responds with a loud firm voice, "Yes sir, I am able."

The news of Joseph's new appointment spread around the house quicker than he expected. It was met with mixed emotions. Some slaves were pleased and happy to work with him, others, especially the Egyptian slaves were not so pleased to have a Hebrew boy as their leader.

A loud voice echoes into the atmosphere - deep, strong, and forceful. His voice is carried with the authority and the responsibility that now belongs to him, Joseph. All he did was utter a simple command. "Leave the bags of grain here for me to count". The other slaves worked quickly to meet his demand.

Joseph stands tall, shoulders straight, like a man of war in the middle of the large courtyard, dressed in new garments, gifts from Potiphar himself. It was more than a month since he assumed his new job as the overseer of Potiphar's household.

He now has much larger living quarters as well as his *own* servants. His new wages mean he can afford some Egyptian luxuries including fine sandals and expensive fragrance oils.

.   .   .

Zuleika looks outside her window, drawn to the sound of Josephs voice. She sees him standing amongst the other slaves. She turns towards her handmaid, who is busy removing dirty linen from the large bed and asks, "Assam, who is that man in the courtyard, the one giving directions to the household?"

Her handmaid rushes to the window and smiles sheepishly at the sight of the man, "It is Joseph my lady, the overseer of the household"

Zuleika, irrationally irritated by the way she sees Assam stare at the man, pulls her away from her the window. "Who is Joseph, is he new to this household? I have never seen him before."

Her other hand maid Ahura walks in to draw her bath and is also called to the window, "Who is that man?"

Her mistress is sickened when Ahura also smiles and says excitedly, "That is Joseph."

Ahura looks at Assam, they both laugh, and Assam looks at her mistress. "He is so handsome my lady, all the slave girls and handmaidens talk about him, we hope he will take a wife from among us and perhaps a few concubines; some have already tried and been dismissed." Assam laughs loudly, pointing at Ahura.

"Back to your chores" Zuleika screams, causing the girls to jump and rush towards their duties. She walks slowly back to the window and stares at Joseph. Can this be the same boy? The slave that her husband had paid a large price for many years ago. Surely, this is not the same scrawny, dirty boy who works in their household? How has he changed so much? This man standing before her has the beauty of a God.

Her mind races as she continues to watch him, and an unwanted desire starts to grow within her. She stares at him longingly, his rich, dark brown hair is shoulder length, combed away from his face, exposing high cheek-bones and a strong jaw. He is dressed in a white garment with navy blue stitching on the shoulders hem. The garment moves and flows with the rise and fall of his chest, showing he is now handsome and well formed. She longs for him to look up towards her, so she can see his face more clearly, a strong desire for him to smile at her causes her to tap on the window.

As if in response, Joseph raises his head, but he doesn't look at her, instead, he looks towards the merchants approaching on the other side of the courtyard and he walks towards them. Zuleika's eyes follow every step until he is out of sight. She smiles and hurries towards the bath Ahura has just drawn. As she steps in, she says to Ahura, "Add some extra oils, bring me the rose oils and put some in my hair as well."

"Ah, rose oils my lady" she winks at her "Will my master be home early tonight?" Ahura teases her.

"Just do as you are told girl," Zuleika snaps at her. She is suddenly irritated by the very thought of her husband.

Ahura is shocked by her mistress's response. They usually talk freely about things of this nature but sensing a change in her mistress she immediately bows her head and does as she is commanded.

Zuleika steps into the large dining room and is greeted by the ladies in the house. As she prepares to set the meal for her husband, Potiphar, her mind wanders to the Hebrew boy who she now longs for. It has been more than nine days since she first saw him and he has occupied her every waking moment, even those where she lay with her husband.

Potiphar returned home, without warning, a week ago on account of Pharaoh. She had hoped that he would be away much longer, to give room for her to seek out Joseph. There has not been one quiet moment with him. She had been careful not to raise any suspicion, especially now she knew that the ladies in the house also desired Joseph. She must be duplicitous, to find a way to be alone with Joseph.

With the table set and the evening meal ready, a call is sent to Potiphar to eat. As he walks in, Joseph follows close behind, both men in deep conversation. A loud crash startles them into raising their heads in unison. Zuleika steps away from the bowl of fresh pomegranate seeds that she held only a few moments ago. "Permit my absence, my lord," she says, bows down to Potiphar and rushes out of the room.

As she walks away to change her soiled garments, she sees Ahura run ahead of her to lay out fresh clothes. Zuleika wipes her head with the back of her left hand. She puts her hand on her chest, trying to cause her heart to stop thundering; the rush of blood to her head from seeing Joseph left her dizzy and confused.

She takes tiny steps, looking down at her feet, forcing her mind to focus. It all happened so fast, she has just made a fool of herself in front of everyone. Joseph is not supposed to be there, he may be an overseer but he is still a Hebrew, it is forbidden for him to eat with the Egyptians. Her thoughts flow freely as she hastens her steps into her living quarters. "I want him so much," she whispers to her reflection. She is now standing in front of the large wooden mirror.

She looks at the new clothes that have been laid out by Ahura and shakes her head. "I would like my chamber clothes please, also, make me a plate of food, I will dine alone tonight. Tell my husband that I am taken with fever".

"Yes, my lady," Ahura responds, nodding her head, walking out of the room, and closing the door gently behind her.

For many months afterwards, Zuleika seizes every opportunity to speak to Joseph, to be around him and in the moments when she is alone with him, she is not ashamed to whisper. "Lie with me." Each time, Joseph makes excuses and leaves quickly, his long stride placing a welcome distance between them. Welcomed by Joseph, that is, not by Zuleika.

It is a cool evening, the sun is hidden by thick pregnant clouds, rain is imminent, and everyone is busy trying to finish their chores before the downpour. Zuleika watches from the large windows in her chambers as the household scurries around, her eyes, firmly fixed on Joseph. He is giving directions; she can't hear his words, but she stares at the movement of his muscular arms, as he points his right hand towards the field.

He turns around unexpectedly, as though responding to his name being called and she wills him to look up, to see her; all he has to do is tilt his head upwards and he will see her, but he doesn't, instead he walks towards the men who had summoned him.

Zuleika lingers at her window, waiting for him to come back. A few moments later, she hears his voice, he is in the house. She picks up her scarf and walks quickly, towards the sound of his voice. She sees him enter her husband's room, the place where all the counting of coins is done, and the affairs of the household are kept.

She slips in quietly, unnoticed and closes the door behind her softly. She walks over to Joseph who is startled by her presence and she places her hand on his mouth so that he doesn't scream. She lets her scarf fall away from her shoulders, showing much more of her skin than is permissible.

The rain is pounding and everyone in the household is scurrying to take cover. Zuleika steps back slowly, now assured he is not going to scream. It is just the two of them. She moves seductively, inviting him to come towards her as she steps back towards the large wool skin rug that lies on a fallen oak tree. "Come Joseph, come and lie with me," she taps on the rug where she is now seated, her eyes fixed on him.

Joseph stands firm, sweat drips down the back of his neck and he swallows twice in quick succession trying to bring some moisture to his now dry mouth. His heart is beating faster than it should, his palms wet but not from the rain outside. He tries to speak but stutters instead making Zuleika chuckle.

"Do your words fail you on account of my beauty, Joseph? And you have not yet touched the softness of my skin. Come and feel it," she whispers, running her hands over her body.

She smiles when she sees Joseph start to move, she inches sideways to give him room to lie down but, instead of coming towards her, he bolts for the door. She jumps to her feet and rushes over to him, blocking his exit. She stares at him, then lifts her right hand and touches his lips gently.

Joseph pushes her hand away and steps back. "I cannot do this thing you are asking of me. This is a wicked thing before my God and before man. My master concerns himself with nothing in this household, everything he owns he has entrusted to my care. There is no one greater than me in this household," Joseph said, pointing his long fingers towards his chest. He takes a few more steps away from her but close enough so she can still hear him in the large room. "Why would I do such a thing to my master? The only thing he has withheld from me is you because you are his wife" He softens his tone on the last words, wanting her to hear him, praying that it will get through to her. He repeats, "You are his wife! I cannot do such a wicked thing and sin against God." He pulls her aside from the door and hurries out without looking back.

Zuleika stands, rubbing her fingers on her arms at the very place Joseph had touched her; she smiles and murmurs, "You will lie with me Joseph." Shaking her head, she walks out the door and down the long path to her chamber on the other side of the house.

~

Twelve Months Later

The noise from the slave girls singing rouses Zuleika from her daydream. They are returning from the festival which she had refused to go to. She quickly grabs some water from the cool pot besides her and splashes it over her head making sure she wets the black Kohl on her eyes causing it to drip on her face.

She starts to scream loudly, gasping for air, holding her head in her hands, and rocking herself back and forth.

Azura reaches her first, "My lady, what has happened?"

Her room is soon filled with slave girls and even some of the men trickle in.

Pointing towards the servant quarters, she gasps for more air, visibly shaken, pretending like she is unable to speak she shakes Joseph's cloak and keeps pointing.

Kamri, one of the Egyptian slaves, the one in charge of the cattle, whispers, "That is Joseph's cloak, why does she have Joseph's cloak?"

Zuleika lifts her head, her eyes red, her face stained black from kohl and water. "That Hebrew slave boy, he tried to rape me." She spat out the words through clenched teeth.

The sound of screaming fills the room and voices whisper, all condemning Joseph.

A few moments later, Potiphar returns to find his house in chaos. He strides through the row of slaves, now lined up and chattering. "What has happened here?" Potiphar's voice booms out. "Where is Joseph?" he demands, wanting to know why his house is not in order.

Zuleika rushes out to meet him and throws herself at his feet, still holding on tightly to Josephs cloak that she had kept beside her while she waited for Potiphar to return. She screams at the top of her voice, "My Lord is this how you are repaid for your kindness? That Hebrew slave, the one you trusted with your household, he tried to defile me. Look at his cloak, he left it behind when I screamed." The lie comes easily as she draws fresh tears from within her, wailing like one bereaved.

Potiphar burns with anger, how has it come to this? He stares at his wife and then looks at his household. All his slaves are gathered waiting for him to act, waiting for him to respond. Joseph is nowhere to be seen. He looks down at Zuleika as she clings to his feet, still crying.

He stares at her with angry silence, his heart breaking quietly within him. For many months, he had watched her watch him. He had observed with silent interest the way she had lusted after his slave boy. He noticed how she no longer argued about his frequent trips anymore, how she welcomed and even tolerated his absence more. He had also watched Joseph, the loyal Hebrew boy who had made him prosper, a boy who had accounted for every coin, every cattle and every grain without any missing.

He knew Joseph was innocent, but he also knew that he needed to act fast to prevent the young man from being killed. It pained him that it had come to this, his wife's betrayal stung and he held back the fury filled tears that threatened to spill.

Many eyes watched him, waiting for his response, waiting for the decree that would see the Hebrew boy murdered. Unwilling to embarrass his wife, and by default himself, and bring shame on his household, Potiphar bellows loudly, "Bring me that slave boy! NOW!"

Zuleika stands up, turning her head slightly into her scarf, and smiles at her victory. How dare he refuse her? She gets herself ready to watch him killed. Disdain and bitterness replace the longing she once held, the lust and deep desire replaced with hatred. She wants him dead. She cannot wait to see him dead.

Joseph is brought in, pushed and spat at by Kamri and Zacceus, the same men he had shared a meal and laughter at daybreak. He frees himself from their grip and walks straight to Potiphar, without looking him in the eyes, he kneels at his feet, his head facing the ground. Closing his eyes, Joseph begins to pray, his life starts to play before, him as he remembers his father, his dreams, his brothers. His tears fall freely, his heart filled with pain and shame. He can hear the whispers of those around him and the words burn deeply into his soul. "Oh God, You know my heart, You know I am innocent, save me," he whispers.

Potiphar stares at the young man before him, "Joseph" he calls loudly.

Joseph looks up at his master and in an instant feels the weight of his right hand as Potiphar strikes him on the face twice in quick succession. Stunned, he falls backwards. From the corner of his bleeding eye, he sees Zuleika smiling. He is sure his death is imminent; he closes his eye, shaking his head slightly to relieve the pain. He can hear Potiphar walking towards him, and he braces himself for the sharp blade that he knows will follow.

Potiphar leans against him, bending down low enough to speak directly into his ear, "Why did you allow this to happen?" He spoke low, for Joseph's ears only. Joseph sits up. Potiphar's words, filled more with disappointment than anger, are confusing.

Potiphar grabs the back of Joseph's hair and lifts him up, tossing him towards Kamri. "Bring round the chariot and have him chained to the back. Take him to the prison, where the king's prisoners are held and leave him there"

Joseph turns to look at Potiphar, briefly catching his eye. He knows his master has spared him. He knows that His God has saved him.

ABOUT THE AUTHOR

Amanda Bedzrah is married to Francois and they have three wonderful children. They live in the county of Kent, best known as "The Garden of England" in the United Kingdom.

Amanda is a passionate Bible teacher, an inspirational speaker, a prayer minister, and a senior NHS professional. She is a Law graduate (LLB Hons), she is also certified in Business Analysis Practice and Project Management.

Find out more:

www.amandabedzrah.com

facebook.com/amandabedzrah
twitter.com/gigidoll2020
instagram.com/Amanda_Bedzrah

ALSO BY AMANDA BEDZRAH

Fiction

Leah: Unnoticed. Unwanted. Unloved

Non – Fiction

The Love that set me free

Overcoming the fear of death

Praying Proverbs

5 Habits of Godly Resilient Women

My Super Power is Kindness (A Journal for Kids)

Choosing Kindness Everyday (A Journal for Teenage Girls & Women)